WE
THE PEOPLE
OSCEOLA

Library of Congress Cataloging-in-Publication Data

Rothaus, James.
  Osceola.

  (We the people)
  Summary: A biography of the Seminole chief who was
both feared and admired by his adversaries for his
efforts to help preserve his people's Florida homeland.
  1. Osceola, Seminole chief, 1804-1838—Juvenile
literature.   2. Seminole Indians—Biography—Juvenile
literature.   3. Seminole Indians—History—Juvenile
literature.   4. Indians of North America—Florida—
History—Juvenile literature.   [1. Osceola, Seminole
Chief, 1804-1838.   2. Seminole Indians—Biography.
3. Indians of North America—Biography]   I. Title.
II. Series: We the people (Mankato, Minn.)
E99.S280845 1987   973'.0497 [B] [92]   87-27147
ISBN 0-88682-162-2

WE
THE PEOPLE
OSCEOLA

SEMINOLE INDIAN WAR CHIEF
(1803-1838)

JAMES R. ROTHAUS

Illustrated By Harold Henriksen And John Keely

CREATIVE EDUCATION

OSCEOLA

In 1813, a ten-year-old Creek Indian youth named Little Boy watched in wonder as a lone warrior rode silently into his village. The warrior was the great Shawnee chief, Tecumseh. He had ridden his spotted pony day and night from faraway Ohio to Little Boy's village in Alabama.

Now Little Boy listened closely as Tecumseh breathlessly spoke his message of war: "White men are taking Indian lands everywhere. They drive red people away or kill them. There are too many white soldiers for one tribe to fight. All Indian people must unite as one.

7

We must take up the hatchet to-gether, or we will all perish."
Then news came to the Creeks that Tecumseh's brother—

The Prophet—had been attacked by white troops at Tippecanoe Creek. Prophet's village had been burned and the Indians driven into the hills.

Enough! The Creek warriors shouted: "Yoho-eelo!" Even Little Boy joined the battle cry. That year, 1813, the Creek War began. Many Creek warriors attacked Fort Mims, Alabama.

Hundreds of settlers around the fort were killed. Then the U.S. government sent General Andrew Jackson and his militia to punish the Creeks. In 1814, Jackson's white soldiers poured into Little Boy's village on the Tallapoosa River. The Creeks fought hard, but they lost the Battle of Horseshoe Bend. Little Boy's father was killed. He

and his mother had to run away.

They fled south toward the wild swamp country of Florida. There, they hoped to find safety among hundreds of Creek, Hitchiti and Apalachee Indians who had already run away from white soldiers in Georgia and Alabama.

The whites hated and feared the fugitive Indians hiding in Florida. They called them "Seminoles," an Indian word meaning "runaways." The whites believed all Indians should simply go meekly to the res-

ervations set aside for them—even though the Indian people had lived in America for thousands of years before the white man came.

Little Boy and his mother braved great hardships on their journey to Florida, but they finally settled in a large village just beyond the white man's Fort Robinson. There, Little Boy grew tall and sturdy.

When he was about 14, Little Boy received his man's name. It happened at the Green Corn Dance, the celebration of the Indians' New Year. Little Boy drank the traditional asi, or black drink. He gave the joyful shout, "Yaholo!" louder than any other boy.

And so he was named Asi-yaholo, or Black Drink Crier. He became the village's most famous athlete. He was a great runner and lacrosse player.

Asi-yaholo grew up and took two wives, as was the Seminole custom. In 1821, when he was about 18, Florida became one of the United States. Its first governor was Andrew Jackson. Like many frontiersmen at the time, Jackson hated the Indians. He said they were savages who stood in the way of white progress. The truth is, Jackson never stopped fighting long enough to study and understand the Indian culture.

Asi-yaholo remembered that Jackson and his militia had killed his father at Horseshoe Bend. Now,

Jackson wanted to send the Seminoles to a strange reservation in the Far West. Then white settlers could take the Indians' farm land. Some of the chiefs were willing to take money and leave. But not Asi-yaholo. He said: "I will not be driven from my home a second time."

Even though he was not a chief, many Indians agreed with Asi-yaholo. In time, he became their leader.

In 1829, Andrew Jackson became President of the United States. By now, he was called "Old Hickory" because he was as tough and strong as a hickory stick. Instead of trying to discuss a just peace with the Seminoles, Jackson insisted they leave Florida. A piece of paper was brought to the Seminole chiefs in 1832. President Jackson called it a treaty, but it was really a demand. If the chiefs signed it, they would agree to go West. If not, they would be *forced* to go West.

Asi-yaholo drew his knife and stabbed the paper. "This is the only way I will sign such a treaty," he said.

From then on the soldiers marked him as an Indian enemy. They called him Osceola.

The white Indian agent, General Wiley Thompson, put Osceola into prison. He was freed only when he said he would sign the treaty. But Osceola later vowed to fight the white invaders.

Other Seminoles who were against moving made Osceola their leader. Entire Seminole villages left their farms and went into the deep swamp.

From there, parties of warriors attacked the white soldiers. When the troops chased the Indians, they hid in the swamp. Osceola was a good general. His Indians beat the whites again and again. He himself killed General Thompson.

Now President Jackson was furious. He was determined to win Florida for the white settlers. He sent one white army after another against Osceola.

Many Seminoles were captured. Others gave up and were sent to Oklahoma. But not Osceola. He

said: "We will fight until the last drop of our blood sinks into these lands of ours."

Was it wrong for Osceola to defend his home? Was it wrong for President Jackson to fight for one of the American states? In their hearts, both leaders—red and white—believed they were right. And so the fighting continued for two years.

Finally, in 1837, white soldiers chased Osceola and his people from

for another parley. Osceola came in under a white flag of truce. He met General Joseph Hernandez, of the Florida militia, near the city of St. Augustine.

Then the Seminoles learned that they would be settled among their old Indian enemies. And the many black people who lived with the Indians would have to stay behind and become white men's slaves.

Osceola said, "These black people have lived with us for many years. They are friends and allies. We will not turn them over to the whites."

The next morning, when the white soldiers awoke, they discovered that all the Indians and the blacks had vanished back into the swamps.

The Seminole War started up again. Osceola's people fought on, despite suffering and want.

Late in 1837, the whites asked

for another parley. Osceola came in under a white flag of truce. He met General Joseph Hernandez, of the Florida militia, near the city of St. Augustine.

their camps before they could harvest crops. Now hunger became the Indians' constant companion. Osceola prayed to the Great Spirit for help.

When General T.S. Jesup sent a message, asking for a parley, Osceola saw it as a sign from God. He quickly agreed to the meeting. He hoped he would be able to work out a way for his people to remain peacefully in Florida. In May, 1837, more than 3,000 Seminoles met Jesup at Fort Brooke on Tampa Bay.

But General Jesup still refused to consider a Seminole reservation in Florida. Once more, he offered the chiefs money if they would move. He had 24 ships ready to take the Indians to the Far West.

General Hernandez suddenly ordered his men to seize Osceola. The Indian leader was hit on the head and tied up. The truce had been a trick. The great Indian leader

had been captured by treachery.

Osceola, sick with malaria, was imprisoned in Fort Marion. He was tired of fighting and he felt that doom hung over his people. A few Indians escaped from the prison, but Osceola was too sick to try.

Osceola was sent to a dungeon in Fort Moultrie, South Carolina. While there, he met a famous white artist named George Catlin. Catlin admired Osceola and wrote about him to the newspapers. People said it was a shame that the Indian had been taken through white treachery. Some said: "Set him free!"

But it was too late. Osceola died of a sickness in January, 1838.

They buried Osceola under a stone that said: PATRIOT AND WARRIOR. But his spirit had not died.

Deep in the swamps, the Seminoles still fought on. Some were captured, but a few escaped into the vast Big Cypress Swamp.

Today, great-grandchildren of these Seminoles still live in Florida. They are the only Indian tribe in the United States that NEVER surrendered.

President Jackson was admired in his day for his fierce determination to rid the state of Florida of the red man. Osceola was also admired by Indians and white people alike for his fierce determination to protect his people and his home. Today, we realize that both men would have been greater in the eyes of history if they had somehow found a way to cease fighting . . . and start talking. This is a lesson that today's leaders are still trying to learn.

WE THE PEOPLE SERIES

WOMEN OF AMERICA

CLARA BARTON
JANE ADDAMS
ELIZABETH BLACKWELL
HARRIET TUBMAN
SUSAN B. ANTHONY
DOLLEY MADISON

INDIANS OF AMERICA

GERONIMO
CRAZY HORSE
CHIEF JOSEPH
PONTIAC
SQUANTO
OSCEOLA

FRONTIERSMEN OF AMERICA

DANIEL BOONE
BUFFALO BILL
JIM BRIDGER
FRANCIS MARION
DAVY CROCKETT
KIT CARSON

WAR HEROES OF AMERICA

JOHN PAUL JONES
PAUL REVERE
ROBERT E. LEE
ULYSSES S. GRANT
SAM HOUSTON
LAFAYETTE

EXPLORERS OF AMERICA

COLUMBUS
LEIF ERICSON
DeSOTO
LEWIS AND CLARK
CHAMPLAIN
CORONADO